COGNITIV
TH

THE BASICS AND BEYOND OF CBT AND PSYCHOTHERAPY

REBECA FRANKS

JB PUBLISHING CO

Cognitive Behavioral Therapy

Cognitive Behavioral Therapy Copyright © 2015 by Rebeca Franks.

All rights reserved. Printed in the United States of America. No part of this book may be used or reproduced in any manner whatsoever without written permission except in the case of brief quotations embodied in critical articles or reviews.

This book contains material protected under International and Federal Copyright Laws and Treaties. Any unauthorized reprint or use of this material is prohibited. No part of this book may be reproduced or transmitted in any form or by any means, electronic or mechanical, including photocopying, recording, or by any information storage and retrieval system without express written permission from the author / publisher.

Any unauthorized broadcasting; public performance, copying or re-recording will constitute an infringement of copyright.

Permission granted to reproduce for personal and educational use only. Commercial copying, hiring, lending is prohibited.

May be used free of charge. Selling without prior written consent prohibited. Obtain permission before redistributing. In all cases this notice must remain intact.

First Edition: August 2015

Cognitive Behavioral Therapy

Cognitive Behavioral Therapy

TABLE OF CONTENTS

Chapter 1: What is CBT? 2

Chapter 2: What Are the Uses of CBT? 9

Chapter 3: History of CBT 23

Chapter 4: Various Methods of CBT 28

Chapter 5: Types of CBT 36

Chapter 6: Criticisms 41

Cognitive Behavioral Therapy

Chapter 1.
What is CBT?

Throughout history, there have been many incredible advances within the discipline of psychology. The way we have come to understand the brain and behavior is truly remarkable and has paved the way for a wide range of therapies. Of course, it wasn't always this way. What many refer to as 'insane asylums,' were the norm for many years.

Patients were exposed to horrendous conditions in order to control their undesirable behaviors. In some cases, holes were drilled into patients heads in order to release evil spirits. It wasn't until the 20th century that psychological breakthroughs were being made. Symptoms of hysteria were eventually treated with hypnosis and various therapies began to take shape.

Freud's psychoanalysis therapy, psychological research, and developing therapy methods gave way to behavioral and cognitive therapy. Originally developed to treat depression, cognitive behavioral therapy (CBT) is one of the few therapies which is scientifically proven to be effective, based on hundreds of clinical trials and practical applications. Basically, **CBT is a form of psychotherapy that focuses on changing behaviors by modifying one's beliefs and distorted thoughts**.

This therapy focuses on the ways in which we perceive situations, directly affecting our feelings and behaviors. If you have a negative interpretation of an event or situation and it goes unchallenged, then you could potentially experience a continuous cycle of thoughts, feelings, and behaviors that are destructive in nature. For some, this affects them throughout the entirety of their lives. As an example, let's focus on a similar scenario affecting two unique and unrelated individuals.

Both Ann and Bob's father left when they were young. Ann has since moved forward and has a family of her own. Although she thinks of her dad, it hasn't affected her mental well-being. Bob, on the other hand, experienced his father leaving and has since felt as though he's worthless. The absence of his father has significantly hurt his self-esteem and is a contributing factor in his persistent anxiety issues.

Although the situations may be unique in terms of the details, the overall past scenario is the same. Both children were not raised by their father, yet their perspectives differ and reactions highly differ. Ann has a more realistic view of her father's absence. Her father leaving was not due to anything she did, therefore she has not punished herself for his actions. Bob has internalized his dad's absence and blames himself. He has the idea that his dad leaving was because he wasn't good enough, leading to all kinds of emotional and interpersonal difficulties in his present life. Bob may not specifically focus on the absence of his father, however, he has carried those negative views of himself throughout his life. Now, they affect his thinking patterns and behaviors.

This is the basis of CBT, as perceived situations are what influence our emotional well-being. This means that it is not necessarily a situation that directly affects how we feel emotionally, rather our thoughts and feelings towards that situation. Ann and Bob experienced the same type of trauma, yet Ann perceived the incident for what it was. However, Bob felt differently and blamed himself. Now he doesn't apply for jobs he wants because he doesn't think he's good enough. This type of thinking patterns is damaging and without cognitive and behavioral interventions, this cycle will continue to control one's thoughts and behaviors.

CBT is all about learning how to stop a cycle of negative thinking and destructive behaviors. By identifying these negative thinking patterns and resulting behaviors, you can change the way you think and behave in the future. As its name states, there are both cognitive and behavioral aspects to this therapy. Cognition focuses on the thoughts that lead to emotional and physical distress. Behaviors, on the other hand, are what worsen and prolong one's negative way of thinking. It's a vicious cycle which is why both aspects need to be addressed. The way you think and behave are not independent of one another. If you change your perspective regarding a specific situation, you could also change your behavior.

As mentioned, the cognitive aspect relates to thinking and one's beliefs. Through the cognitive aspect of therapy, patients learn new methods and skills, in order to change their current thinking patterns. For example, a woman may seek therapy for depression. She has low self-esteem and often expresses that she's worthless. Through cognitive therapy, the client would learn to interpret her automatic thought of 'being worthless' and replace it with more positive thoughts, such as 'I have value.' Any thoughts that are contributing to her low self-esteem would be addressed.

Behavioral is, of course, what we do. When a client takes part in cognitive behavioral therapy, they will address unhealthy and problematic behaviors, replacing them with healthier responses. This aspect of therapy is concerned with practical everyday situations based on what's learned in therapy. For example, a man may be seeking CBT while recovering from alcohol addiction. Together, the therapist and client would develop strategies to overcome impulses that may cause him to drink, based on his identified triggers. The client would learn new coping skills which would be practiced and strengthened. Whether it may be avoiding certain social situations or substituting drinking for a less harmful behavior, the implied coping skills would be based on the individual's personal situation and condition.

Lastly, some therapists are beginning to incorporate some emotional strategies. Working with emotion has been a weakness within CBT in the past, but is now used by some therapists to help clients become more calm, relaxed, and de-stressed. By implementing emotional strategies, the mind can stay more relaxed and is more receptive to therapy. Depending on the scenario, client's may benefit from mindfulness, acceptance and compassion-based techniques, and/or imagery.

A key characteristic of CBT is that it's fairly short-lived. This is a great advantage in terms of recovery. Not only do clients recover more rapidly, but they're able to maintain and manage their recovery long-term. It was originally designed to be a quick and practical treatment option, providing patients with long-term skills to support their health. When taking part in CBT, patients focus on the present moment. Clients are asked to address the issues that create challenges in their day-to-day life. This helps individuals reflect, so that they can properly interpret the world around them and how it affects their thoughts and behaviors.

While focusing on CBT as a whole, there are two critical components – functional analysis and skills training. Functional analysis plays a crucial role in helping both the client and therapist assess high-risk triggers and situations that lead to problematic behaviors and thoughts. Based on this analysis, clients are introduced to skills training. Learning plays a key role in CBT which is why clients are encouraged to *unlearn* old behaviors and *learn* new ones.

After all, CBT is based on social learning which is why learning and unlearning are key focal points. Depending on the situation, a mixture of techniques may be used such as modeling, as well operant and/or classical conditioning. To summarize, here are the key characteristics of cognitive behavioral therapy:

- Based on a cognitive model of emotional responses. **It is one's thoughts that create**

their feelings and behaviors, not the external world around them. This means that even if a situation does not change, individuals can change the way they think and respond.

- **It is short-lived, yielding faster results**. On average (across all conditions), clients receive around sixteen sessions. In comparison to other therapies that can potentially take years, CBT is time-limited. It's meant to address issues, build new coping skills and strategies, creating long-term, lasting results.

- **A strong relationship between the therapist and client is required** in order for therapy to be effective. Within CBT this trusting relationship is important, however, it's not enough to truly create lasting results. Along with a positive relationship, CBT therapists will focus on teaching self-counseling skills as well. These skills are what help clients think differently long-term.

- **CBT does not tell people how they should feel but rather teaches them the benefits of feeling calm when confronted with distressing situations.** It emphasizes the fact that a problem will exist whether you react poorly to it or not. If an individual becomes increasingly upset or anxious, they then have two problems. The problem itself and their feelings about it.

- When taking part in CBT, **it is highly structured and focused**, as therapists will have a specific agenda planned for each session. Clients will have goals and this direct and structured approach allows them to achieves those goals. CBT therapists will not tell their clients *what* to do, rather teach them *how* to do it. Instead of telling them to feel better, they teach them strategies that will assist them in doing so. It is a highly collaborative approach, as therapists listen, encourage and teach while clients need to express themselves, learn, and implement what they've learned to improve.

- CBT is not focused on 'just talking' as this therapy is scientifically supported in terms of learned emotions and behaviors. **CBT teaches individuals how to unlearn undesirable reactions and to relearn more productive and healthy reactions**. In turn, this leads to long-term results, not just short-term comfort.

These characteristics have helped many individuals based on a variety of advantages. CBT can be as effective as medication when treating certain disorders. Mild depression, for instance, can possibly be treated with CBT alone. It has also shown to be effective in cases where medication alone had not worked.

1. Since CBT is highly structured, it can be provided in various formats, including self-help books, computer programs, and in group settings. The skills that are learned throughout therapy are practical and can be incorporated into everyday life. This helps individuals cope better in terms of future triggers and stressors

Chapter 2.
What are the uses of CBT

As mentioned, CBT was originally developed to treat depression. Today, it has a wide range of applications, treating all types of mental health conditions. Anything from specific phobias and anxiety, to substance abuse and anger issues. Since CBT is so widely used and accepted today, it's even being used in terms of medically related disorders, such as cancer, chronic pain, or premenstrual syndrome. Although this is not a complete list, here are some of the disorders that have been successfully treated by CBT:

- Major depressive disorder
- Generalized anxiety disorder
- Panic disorder
- Social phobia
- OCD
- Conduct disorder
- Substance abuse
- ADD/ADHD
- Eating disorders
- Personality disorders
- Bipolar (with medication)
- Schizophrenia (with medication)
- Family and couples problems
- Pathological gambling
- Anger
- Caregiver distress
- Chronic back pain
- Cancer pain

- Obesity
- Insomnia
- Hypertension
- Erectile dysfunction
- Chronic fatigue syndrome
- And more

There's most certainly a wide range of possibilities and applications, however, we're going to specifically focus on:

- **Panic and anxiety disorders**
- **Obsessive compulsive disorder (OCD)**
- **Mood disorders, such as bipolar and depression**
- **Eating disorders**
- **Post-traumatic stress disorder (PTSD)**
- **Alcohol and drug misuse**
- **Obesity**

PANIC AND ANXIETY DISORDERS

When it comes to anxiety disorders, CBT aims to help an individual develop a more controlled response to their fears. For some, a panic or anxiety disorder can be crippling. Symptoms can often feel as though they surface out of the blue, however, they're actually a product of one's own thoughts. This is why CBT is so effective. Once these thoughts are broken down, individuals begin to master them and gain control.

First, individuals need to identify their distorted thought patterns that create anxiety in the first place. A classic example is a fear of heights. For someone that suffers from a panic disorder, looking over a balcony could create immense fear, causing high levels of panic. CBT allows the individual to really unravel their thoughts and fears so that they can change their distorted way of thinking.

At this point, a therapist may use exposure therapy. In a safe and comforting environment, the individual will be exposed to their panic and anxiety-related fears. The main goal would be to lessen one's anxiety over time based on this gradual exposure. As one is exposed, their sensitivity drops and they learn not to fear a once problematic situation. It's also a great tool to help cope with traumatic memories.

To recap, the cognitive component helps identify the thinking patterns that trigger one's anxiety while the behavioral component involves exposure and desensitization. If someone is fearful of flying, they could begin by making a list of their fears involving flying. Then, they will take steps to improve their overall anxiety levels. They may start by looking at pictures of planes, followed by watching planes at the airport, and then flying themselves.

MOOD DISORDERS

Everyone experiences up and downs throughout life. For healthy individuals, they're able to face upsetting people and situations, rebounding and then finding emotional balance. For those that suffer from a mood disorder, they're often experiencing a constant battle. Mood disorders can take on various forms and include:

- Chronic mild to moderate depression

- Major depressive disorder

- Mania or bipolar disorder

- Depression due to substance abuse

When focusing on minor or moderate depression, CBT has been shown to be particularly effective. For some, their symptoms have been treated with just CBT alone. Others required a combination of therapies or CBT and medication treatment. Individuals learn to recognize defeating thought patterns and then replace them with healthier beliefs.

When someone is suffering from depression, CBT can once again help them analyze their negative thinking patterns. This is a great tool, as it allows patients to focus on being more realistic and positive in their ways of thinking. They're able to recognize the triggers that manifest their destructive thoughts so that they can effectively intervene. While working with a therapist, individuals will focus on thought patterns such as:

- Black and white thinking

- Wrongfully generalizing situations based on negative thoughts

- Exaggerating circumstances with a negative approach

- Automatically forming snap conclusions based on their negative emotions

- Not recognizing or appreciating the positive aspects to a situation

- Assuming that the worst will happen

Bipolar is another prime example, however, many individuals often rely on medications as well. CBT is mainly used as a supportive and additional treatment options. The medication helps stabilize changes in mood so that they're more receptive to the therapy they receive. The key is learning what triggers change their mood and recognizing when these shifts in mood are about to occur. Through CBT, many bipolar individuals are able to avoid significant relapse.

OBSESSIVE-COMPULSIVE DISORDER

For many years, the treatment of obsessive-compulsive disorder (OCD) was believed to be quite difficult. In fact, it was regarded as chronic and untreatable. Within the past fifteen years or so, developments in CBT have created beneficial OCD treatment options.

So, how exactly is CBT effective?

For starters, it's highly structured which is beneficial in terms of chaotic thoughts and perceptions. It's both problem and goal-oriented, really allowing individuals to examine their destructive thoughts and reach their goals. Within

OCD treatment, CBT teaches individuals strategies and skills that can be used long-term, supporting lasting results. When it comes to individuals with OCD, there are two distinct areas of CBT treatment. The first is *exposure and response prevention (ERP)* while the second is *cognitive therapy*.

Like the fear of flying example, we discussed earlier, exposure and response prevention (ERP) is the most widely practiced behavior therapy for OCD. The exposure portion of treatment focuses on either imagined or direct exposure to situations or objects that trigger feelings of anxiety. As time progresses, anxiety decreases based on gradual exposure. This is what's known as *habituation*, the process of getting used to a certain cue or trigger.

The response aspect of treatment refers to the behaviors that individuals with OCD engage in when attempting to reduce anxiety. For some, this may mean washing their hands a hundred times a day. Individuals learn how to avoid these ritualistic behaviors, eventually discontinuing their engagement altogether.

Here is an example of how this treatment works. First, individuals make a list of the situations and things that create feelings of fear and anxiety. Someone who is fearful of germs and contamination, may create a list that includes touching door handles, using toilets, shaking hands, or any other situation that they struggle with.

Treatment begins by exposing individuals to situations that cause mild to moderate levels of anxiety. As progress is made, these individuals graduate to instances that create greater levels of anxiety. The time it takes to progress is dependent on the individual, their ability to tolerate anxiety, and their ability to resist the obsessive behaviors they often take part in. Even those who have severe and long-standing OCD symptoms often benefit from exposure and response prevention. The individual's level of motivation is a large contributing factor here in terms of successful and lasting results.

Since individuals with OCD become anxious based on their thoughts, it can create undesirable behaviors that are overwhelming and constant. For someone that is fearful to leave the house because of a possible fire, they may check over and over again that appliances are unplugged and that the stove is turned off. This is when cognitive therapy is generally used, in combination with ERP.

While participating in exposure tasks, they're often asked to pay attention to their specific emotions, thoughts, and feelings based on the situation. If someone fears shaking hands, for instance, they may express the fear that they'll become ill. Based on these thoughts, this idea can then be challenged so that it no longer creates anxiety or is viewed as a high-risk activity.

Cognitive therapy helps clients really analyze their beliefs and consider the potential consequences of either engaging or not engaging in their obsessive behaviors. The goal is working towards eliminating this compulsive behavior. If someone washes their hands continually for a certain amount of time, they may believe that this protects them against germs. However, once their beliefs are challenged and shown to be false, this can help correct and control these problematic behaviors. It's critical for clients to exchange unrealistic thought patterns with more realistic ideas regarding a high-anxiety situation.

A beneficial tool used is a *thought record*. Within a thought record, participants record their obsessions and their interpretations of those obsessions. When a destructive thought or idea is experienced, clients are asked to record details, such as where they were, what the thoughts or ideas entailed, what the possible meaning could be, and what the individual did. By implementing both exposure exercises and cognitive therapy, individuals highly benefit in terms of their overall thoughts and behaviors.

EATING DISORDERS

Eating disorders are a very real and serious condition. Without intervention, many individuals will put their health at significant risk. Since CBT is based on the fact that one's emotions, thoughts, and behaviors can be restructured to support healthier beliefs and actions, it is the perfect therapy for many individuals.

When it comes to cognitive factors, an eating disorder can cause an individual to over evaluate their body shape and weight. With this comes a negative body image and a decrease in self-worth. Striving for perfectionism based on unrealistic beliefs drives this disease. In terms of behavioral factors, individuals focus on behaviors that control their weight. This will be anything from restricting their diet to binging and purging. Some will even take part in self-harm or obsessive body checking and body avoidance.

These thoughts and behaviors are often based on negative and distorted views that the individuals have of themselves. These distorted thoughts then trigger feelings of shame, guilt, and anxiety which are followed by weight control behaviors. This creates a cycle that is destructive in nature, especially in terms of one's physical and mental health.

Through CBT, individuals with eating disorders are asked to address specific triggers and factors that drive their disorder. They're then asked to address these factors by setting personal goals throughout the various phases of CBT.

CBT often uses skills training as well as education techniques in order for the individual to gain true insight. Understanding oneself as well as the eating disorder itself, helps individuals heal. In the first phase, behaviors are typically addressed. While working on stabilizing eating-related symptoms, emotions can often intensify. During this phase, patients are provided with tools to help them cope and manage their feelings. These individuals are often given homework, allowing them to practice their newly learned skills.

The next phase is the cognitive phase, where restructuring techniques are implemented. An example of this would be changing certain thought processes and patterns of thinking that lead to destructive behaviors. Any beliefs that fuel one's eating disorder are addressed, as these beliefs often perpetuate problems. If required, some therapists will discuss broader issues as well, such as relationships, emotional regulation, self-esteem, and body issues.

Last, individuals focus on relapse prevention. Triggers are reduced while individuals maintain the progress they have made in therapy. Although symptom reduction is a key goal, the main goal is assisting the patient in terms of their physical and emotional well-being. It's critical that individuals return to a healthy and fulfilling life.

POST-TRAUMATIC STRESS DISORDER

Post-traumatic stress disorder (PTSD) can make dealing with the past and present extremely challenging. Instead of expressing how one feels, emotions and thoughts are often bottled up. By taking part in CBT, clients can really benefit. Research has shown that CBT is actually the most effective type of therapy when dealing with PTSD and its related symptoms.

While treating this condition, a therapist helps the individual understand the traumatic events that have occurred and change the way they think based on its aftermath. The main goal is understanding how specific thoughts relating to the trauma cause stress and make symptoms worse. With the help of a therapist, these thoughts are replaced with more accurate thoughts that are less distressing.

Individuals are also taught how to effectively cope with their feelings of fear, guilt, shame, and anger. A soldier, for instance, may feel overwhelmingly guilty that their friend was killed in the line of duty. Cognitive therapy helps many soldiers understand that the traumatic event they experienced was not their fault.

Once again, exposure therapy is often used to lessen the fear associated with these troubling memories. It's all about gaining control over one's thoughts and feelings. In turn, this helps individuals change how they react within a certain situation. Often individuals discuss memories that are less upsetting first, before opening up about the worst and most traumatic events. This is what's known as *desensitization* and it allows individuals to deal with distressing memories gradually. In some cases, therapists also ask their clients to remember many bad memories all at once. This is what's referred to as *flooding* and helps clients to cope more effectively, learning not to become overwhelmed.

SUBSTANCE ABUSE DISORDERS

Addiction directly affects millions each and every day. Not only are addicts struggling to recover, but their family members witness their addiction and fear for their well-being. Within many recovery centers, CBT is offered as an effective treatment option based on the positive results many have experienced.

For those that struggle with substance abuse, it is common for them to display negative and destructive thinking patterns. When these unhealthy thought patterns are not recognized, individuals often experience co-morbid conditions, such as depression or anxiety disorders. In order to fully treat many clients in recovery, both their addiction and any underlying conditions need to be addressed. CBT targets harmful thinking patterns and helps clients change distressing emotions and harmful behavior.

When it comes to substance abuse, CBT is the perfect solution as it is present-oriented, goal-directed, and problem-focused. By exploring one's patterns of behavior, their beliefs can be identified in relation to their actions. This leads to the therapist and client working together in order to seek alternate thinking patterns. Like many other conditions, clients will often receive homework to complete between sessions.

CBT directly challenges an individual's negative or distorted thinking which often drives their addiction. Their cognitive tendencies are deep-rooted and ingrained in themselves, making it challenging to reach a more stable mental health and refrain from using. By changing one's thinking, alternative behavior skills are implemented into their treatment plan.

CBT has applications in both group and individual therapy. Often clients are taught new skills within individual sessions, then are able to practice them in a safe group environment. These skills will be practical and useful so that they can be incorporated into everyday life situations. When everyone in a group can relate to one another, this can provide an excellent support system. Support is critical as clients will need to actively use their new coping skills to handle potential stressors in their lives as they nurture their recovery.

OBESITY

CBT is useful in treating obesity, as it involve behaviors and thinking patterns that affect daily functioning. Since CBT breaks these negative cycles, it can be life-changing for those involved. Although CBT alone will not help individual lose weight, it's meant to be a supportive tool as lifestyle changes are implemented. By taking part in cognitive and behavioral-based therapy, overweight individuals can benefit by:

- Learning to control their diet and becoming more motivated to exercise

- Develop coping skills that will help individuals deal with potential lapses in their diet

- Changing an individual's body image and their expectations surrounding their body

- Improving their self-esteem

- Helping to reduce stress, aiding in potential comfort eating

- Helping individual's set reasonable goals as they build long-term weight maintenance skills

Once someone decides that they'd like to lose weight, CBT can help them along the way. The very first step will be making lifestyle changes. This will focus on their diet and level of exercise. Once these changes are in place, it's critical to address any potential problems that may cause the individual to abandon their weight-loss plan. If someone binge eats in response to their mood (comfort eating), CBT could help solve this issue. By positively influencing one's mood, they will be able to reduce their urges to comfort eat.

Next, many individuals need to address their self-esteem and body image. Our society has created unrealistic goals for many. It's more about becoming healthy than obtaining their ideal 'perfect' body. CBT can address issues surrounding one's body image and make them realize that there's more to a person than how they appear to others. More importantly, CBT can help address how one views themselves. In turn, goals will be set and maintenance will be continually addressed based on self-counseling techniques learned in therapy.

Chapter 3. History of CBT

For many years, therapy was mainly focused on psychoanalysis. It wasn't until the 1940s that a need for effective short-term treatment developed. It was during this time that WWII vets were returning home with severe cases of anxiety and depression.

Based on this need and the behavioral research that had been collected over the past few decades, behavior therapy would soon be born. Cognitive advances were not made until shortly after. This created a revolution in the field of mental health throughout the 1960s which eventually shaped cognitive behavioral therapy, providing us with many of the therapy options used today. So, how did this common therapy come to be?

Based on Freud's therapies and theories, cognitive and behavioral therapy yielded significant changes within psychology and traditional therapy. This was partially due to advances in the way we understood the neurological and biochemical functioning in the brain. Also, many therapists were simply frustrated with the limitations of the most prevalent therapists during this time.

The 'first wave' of CBT has roots in behavior therapy, especially regarding Ivan Pavlov's work on learning and classical conditioning. Throughout the 1950s and 1960s, many behavioral techniques were used, such as B.F Skinner's work regarding operant conditioning, Rotter and Bandura's work on social learning theory, and Wolpe's work on desensitization. Soon, cognitive therapy began to develop. Unlike the work of Freud, cognitive therapists were more interested in the conscious mind in present time. For many years, issues such as anxiety and depression were linked to unconscious memories and emotions. Cognitive therapists began talking to their patients about their thoughts and beliefs and helped them fix these problematic ideas.

One of the first therapists to address cognition in terms of psychotherapy was Alfred Adler. He recognized that basic mistakes played a role in unhealthy emotions. Adler's work is what ultimately influenced the work of Ellis, who developed one of the earliest forms of cognitive-based psychotherapy.

In 1955, Albert Ellis, Ph.D., developed rational emotive therapy. This therapy is the pioneering form of CBT. He believed that psychoanalysis was not effective or direct in nature. There have been philosophic reflections which strongly support RET throughout history. For instance, Epictetus wrote, *'men are disturbed not by things, but by the view which they take them.'* Amazingly, this book known as *The Enchiridion* was published in 125 AD.

Ellis than developed the popular ABC model of emotion which was later changed to the A-B-C-D-E approach. It wasn't until the 1990s that Ellis renamed this approach to rational emotive behavior therapy (REBT). Around the same time that rational emotive therapy (as it was called in the late 1950s) was developed, Aaron Beck began conducting his own research. Today, both Beck and Ellis are regarded as the founding fathers of cognitive behavioral practices.

Aaron Beck, M.D., developed cognitive therapy in the 1960s. He was a scientist at heart and believed that in order for psychotherapy to be widely accepted, he needed to demonstrate its validity. His goal was to perform experiments in order to reach this validation, however, his results showed the opposite of what he'd expect.

For his test, he decided to analyze depressed patients dreams. He predicted that dreams would manifest into themes of hostility, based on the psychoanalytic concept that depression is related to hostility felt towards oneself. Instead, he found that depressed patients actually showed fewer themes of hostility and more feelings of loss and deprivation. Based on his results, he began to look for further explanations regarding depression.

He recognized that his patients' dreams were paralleled to the thinking patterns they experienced while they were awake. In 1967, he started to believe that depressed patients did not need to suffer and that there was a better way to treat their symptoms. He started recognizing a pattern of negative thoughts across his patients and began helping them evaluate and improve their unrealistic thoughts. When he did so, they rapidly improved.

Dr. Beck and A. John Rush conducted the first outcome trail. They both agreed that their study was necessary for determining the effectiveness of CBT. Their randomized controlled study of depressed patients was published in 1977, showing that CBT was as effective as a common antidepressant at the time, known as imipramine. This was very exciting, as it was the first time that a form of talk therapy could be compared to medication. Two years later, in 1979, the first cognitive therapy treatment manual was published.

In the late 1970s, Beck and post-doctoral individuals at the University of Pennsylvania began to study anxiety. Unlike depression, they found that they needed to take a somewhat different approach. Patients who showed signs of anxiety needed to assess the situations they feared in order to improve.

Cognitive therapy was a highly effective treatment option for those that suffered from depression and quickly became well respected. It was these two key therapies, rational emotive therapy, and cognitive therapy, that gave way to the 'second wave' of CBT.

Behavioral approaches had been successful in treating neurotic disorders but made little progress in treating depression. Based on the cognitive revolution, behaviorism was also losing popularity. During the 1980s and 1990s, these two therapy options began to merge. Excitingly, this merging created the successful development of panic disorder treatment. There have been a number of forms that have influenced CBT which all share common characteristics with Beck's therapy, however, they vary slightly. Some of these include:

- Cognitive behavior modification was developed by Meichenbaum in 1977

- Lineham developed dialectical behavior therapy in 1993

- Exposure therapy was developed in 1998 by Foa and Rothbaum

- D'Zurilla and Nezu developed problem-solving therapy in 2006

These are just some of the alternate forms that have been offered in the past and are continually used today. Due to the therapeutic success seen from CBT as well as experimental support, it has become widespread today. Some argue that it is, in fact, the more effective and efficient form of therapy offered today. There are various therapies offered now, which blend elements of cognitive and behavioral treatment and are considered to be the 'third and current wave' of CBT.

Since many CBT psychologists have made it their life work to prove the effectiveness of their therapy techniques, there have been more clinical trails centered around CBT in recent years, than any other form of therapy. It has also shown to be effective across a wide range of emotional issues, from mood disorders to food and substance-related disorders, to anger and OCD, as well as trauma and insomnia.

Today, hundreds of studies have demonstrated the efficacy of CBT based on a wide range of psychological and medical problems with a psychological component. CBT is now taught in most graduate schools within the United States and throughout many other countries across the world.

Chapter 4.
Various Methods of CBT

When it comes to CBT methods, there are various techniques that are used today. By implementing different methods, cognitive behavioral therapists are able to use changes in behavior, mood, cognitions, and even physiology.

These techniques can be environmental, cognitive, behavioral, supportive, experimental, biological, or interpersonal. Depending on one's personal needs and goals, therapists select specific techniques which will benefit that individual. The methods used will also depend on the condition that's being treated.

Let's focus on depression for a moment. Individuals who suffer from depression fixate on negative emotions, not allowing themselves to benefit from positive ones. When taking part in regular CBT sessions, individuals can recognize negative thoughts, then leave them behind. Here are some core examples of ways in which a therapist may work with a depressed patient.

The first step would be locating and understanding what the issue truly is and then brainstorming potential solutions. Depending on the individual, they may benefit from different methods. For some, talking is the best way to uncover their true thoughts and feelings, while others respond better to journaling. If someone is overly lonely, then there are steps to take in order to relieve depressive feelings. Action steps could include volunteering in the community, online dating, or joining a local club. This helps reduce feelings of hopelessness. Depending on a number of factors, clients can access therapy through the following methods.

THERAPIST

When it comes to CBT, the relationship one has between themselves and their therapist is important. A typical CBT session would allow a patient to be face-to-face with their therapist, as they build a trusting bond. Depending on the condition and severity, patients generally take part in anywhere from 6-18 sessions.

Since these sessions are often spread out with a gap of 1-3 weeks between sessions, therapists provide homework assignments for their patients. Based on their goals and the skills they've learned, they're asked to complete various assignments before their next session. This not only shows that a patient wants to change but is willing to change.

For someone with anxiety, for instance, their homework assignment may be as simple as going to a social gathering and meeting one new person. Based on how well an assignment goes, it will influence the next step within their treatment. Unlike many therapy options, the patient is very much involved in CBT. Instead of acting as an authority figure, a CBT therapist is fairly flexible, listening to the patients needs and concerns.

Depending on a client's specific needs and treatment plan, their therapist may utilize a number of techniques. It's important to understand that CBT techniques come in all shapes and sizes, offering varying methods to fit a certain preference. Some of these techniques include behavioral experiments, thought records, pleasant activity scheduling, or exposure.

Exposure Techniques

A therapist may use imagery-based exposure, situation-based exposure, or both. For situation exposure, therapists often ask their clients to make a list of situations or things that they would normally avoid. These should be listed in a hierarchy, as some instances will be more distressing than others. For someone with an eating disorder, for instance, ice cream or chips may be a 10 while grapes may be a 2. For someone with social anxiety, asking someone on a date may yield a rating of 10, while asking someone directions could be a 5. The list would then be rated from highest to lowest, with the list clearly showing what the main issue is.

A list is created so that clients may begin to face their fears, starting with the fear that creates the amount of least anxiety or distress. The idea is to expose the client to their list of distressing items until the amount of distress experienced is significantly reduced. This can also be done within imagery-based exposure and has the client visualize instances of distress, reporting the emotions and behaviors that follow. The client is asked to visualize the distressing event in detail until their distress levels are reduced.

Behavioral Experiments

Within CBT, behavioral experiments are designed to test one's thoughts. These planned activities are based on experimentation or observation. They are used to test existing beliefs, as they're often old, unhelpful, and negative. In turn, these experiments can also test a client's new beliefs in order to compare results.

This is a great tool used with CBT, as it helps clients to engage in a way that's not just verbal. Based on adult learning theories, it's important to experience and reflect. When clients are exposed to these experiments, it creates a deeper level of information processing.

If someone is a perfectionist to the point where they experience anxiety. They will be asked to try an experiment planned by their therapist, then test the consequences. The purpose here is to show individuals that your thoughts and feelings create behaviors, however, your behaviors also create new thoughts and emotions.

For some, this may be experimenting with a friend, telling them that they made some sort of mistake. As a perfectionist, this would be challenging. However, once they see that their friend doesn't think any differently, their anxiety is slightly reduced. The overall goal is to show the clients that nothing catastrophic will happen. This may help an individual see that being perfect is less important than they previously thought. There has been plenty of evidence suggesting that changing behaviors are often one of the most effective ways to change both thoughts and feelings.

Thought Records

Like behavioral experiments, thought records are meant to test the validity of one's thoughts and feelings. Thought records help challenge thoughts that aren't realistic, helping to make positive changes. This requires an individual to look at a situation from two sides. What evidence is there that their thoughts are accurate and what evidence shows that they may not be accurate in their beliefs?

Individuals can record their thoughts in a chart, really focusing on the situation and the evidence surrounding that specific issue. Clients would write where they were, how they were feeling, the negative thought that caused distress, the evidence that supports that thought, evidence that does not support that thought, a possible alternative thought, and then the emotion that follows.

Here is an example:

The situation. While at work, Sue made a mistake within some paperwork. She is feeling anxious that her boss will now think she's a failure.

Initial thought. This focuses on what Sue initially thought when she made a mistake. This is when she relates to herself as a failure, thinking that no one will like her based on her mistakes.

Negative thinking. By Sue self-labeling herself as a failure, she's assuming that her boss and everyone at work will think she's also a failure.

Supporting evidence. To support the fact that Sue's a 'failure,' she may think *I'm often hard on myself*.

Non-supporting evidence. Sue should focus on the fact that her boss has given her positive feedback all week. He's also allowing her to run a staff meeting next week. If he thought she was a failure or useless, would he provide positive feedback and give her more responsibility? This is where Sue needs to challenge her way of thinking.

An alternative thought. Sue then writes down in her thought record chart that she doesn't always need to be perfect. People make mistakes, however, she knows she can make up for it. She may think, *I can learn from my mistakes, I am not a failure, and I am too hard on myself*.

An emotion. She may feel positive in that she's not a failure. The next time she makes a mistake, she will not dwell on it and instead, she'll focus on learning from that situation and continually succeeding like she has in the past.

Pleasant Activity Scheduling

This technique is especially useful in terms of depression. Therapists ask their clients to write down seven days, then schedule one pleasant activity per day. This can be anything that they enjoy that's not unhealthy (going drinking for example, would not be an acceptable choice). This can be as simple as reading a chapter from their favorite book, sitting down for a nice lunch at work without rushing, or going to see a movie with a friend. For some, they may alter this technique to schedule instances that will yield a sense of accomplishment or competence.

COMPUTERIZED

For some, they benefit more from an interactive computer-based CBT. Not everyone can afford or has access to a human therapist, however, computerized cognitive behavioral therapy (CCBT) is allowing for greater access to evidence-based therapies. In real-life, patients are not always receiving the evidence-based therapy within routine care. Unfortunately, long waiting times for therapy, reduced accessibility, and service costs are a reality for many individuals in need of therapy.

In response to these challenges, alternative methods were created. This is especially effective when treating mild or moderate depression and anxiety. Computer software programs are being used to treat a wide range of mental health conditions, leading to both advantages and disadvantages.

In terms of advantages, CCBT is more cost-effective and allows greater access to therapy options. Since CCBT can be done at home, it's delivered to this setting rapidly. Also, CCBT is a highly client-lead treatment option, so it can actually promote control, mastery, and learned resourcefulness. Some view this lack of face-to-face treatment as a disadvantage, as well as a potential safety concern.

With advances in Internet functions, instead of face-to-face communication with a therapist, patients utilize an interactive voice response system. This is also known as internet-delivered cognitive behavioral therapy (ICBT). Internet-based programs have several advantages in comparison to stand-alone computer programs. Since the Internet is constantly available, it allows individuals to access treatment from a range of locations. Information can also be presented in a number of languages, styles, or formats, based on the learning preferences or strengths of the user. Either way, CCBT and ICBT are most certainly growing interest and expanding evidence is supporting this method of therapy.

SELF-HELP AND SELF-MONITORING

Self-help can be very powerful. There are multiple strategies regarding self-monitoring. Writing down one's thoughts so that they can properly reflect is a key example. Some other forms are monitoring symptoms, rating mood on a daily basis, and scheduling activities with a clear goal in mind.

When keeping track of one's thoughts and experiences on a day-to-day basis, the individual can instantly become more self-aware. Based on their records, they can pinpoint situations that triggered feelings of distress. If you were to do this, you may find that there are common similarities between events that you were not even aware of. This is also a great way to understand the ways in which certain events and situations affect mood and well-being.

Within therapy, many benefit from exposure therapy, especially when dealing with instances of anxiety. The idea behind this therapy is that exposure helps to reduce one's fear of specific situations or things. When individuals are gradually exposed to whatever creates anxiety for them, they see that their fears are irrational. Anxiety begins to slowly decrease until the individual is able to significantly reduce feelings of fear and anxiety, allowing them to regain control. These new skills developed within therapy can then be applied within the client's everyday life.

Chapter 5. Types of CBT

Technically speaking, cognitive behavioral therapy is a blend of both behavioral therapy and cognitive therapy. Today, cognitive behavioral therapy is an umbrella term for a wide range of related therapy options. These therapies include, but are not limited to:

- **Brief CBT**
- **Dialectical Behavior Therapy**
- **REBT**
- **Interpersonal therapy**
- **Family-focused therapy**
- **Stress Inoculation Training**

BRIEF CBT

Originally developed and implemented for soldiers overseas, brief CBT is only meant to last for a couple of sessions, lasting up to 12 accumulated hours. Clients start with an orientation, covering topics such as one's commitment to treatment, treatment journals, crisis response, a model of suicidality, and more.

Next, the main focus is skill building. Clients are given skill development worksheets and coping cards. Demonstrations are given so that clients can put their new skills into practice. Once practiced, these skills are refined. Last, relapse presentation is targeted.

DIALECTICAL BEHAVIOR THERAPY

Dialectical behavior therapy (DBT), is a type of CBT first developed by Marsha Linehan. When first developed, it was intended to treat individuals who were suffering from suicidal thoughts and tendencies. It is also now used to treat individuals who suffer from borderline personality disorder (BPD), as this illness often displays suicidal symptoms.

The core concept behind this therapy is to take two opposing views and blending them together. The views will be two extremes, yet individuals will be encouraged to meet somewhere in the middle. Although their feelings may be valid, the therapist teaches the individual that they're responsible for their destructive behavior and unhealthy thought processes.

Although the therapist will emphasize an equal relationship in terms of a patient and therapist, they will also consistently remind them to recognize their disruptive thoughts and actions. Then, coping skills and healthier coping mechanisms are introduced. Within individual therapy, these skills are taught and understood while group therapy allows individuals to put these skills into action. It's a safe place to practice their budding skills in order to improve.

Rational Emotive Behavior Therapy (REBT)

Albert Ellis developed a type of cognitive-behavioral therapy known as rational emotive behavior therapy (REBT) to help individuals change their irrational beliefs. This began with the ABC Model, suggesting that people irrationally blame external events for their lack of happiness. Ellis argued that it is not these events but our interpretation of events that leads to psychological distress. The ABC Model refers to:

A – Activating Event. This means that something occurs within your environment.

B- Beliefs. You then have a belief based upon that situation or event.

C- Consequence. Based on your belief, you have an emotional response.

By identifying these irrational beliefs, you can then challenge them. When someone has such rigid beliefs or thoughts, it is impossible to respond in a psychologically healthy way. Once they have been identified, the patient is then encouraged to challenge these mistaken beliefs. Unlike many therapy options where the therapist is supportive and warm, REBT requires them to be blunt, logical, direct, and honest.

INTERPERSONAL THERAPY

Like CBT, interpersonal therapy does not aim to change one's personality or adjust everything that's going on their life. Instead, it aims to solve problems that are in the present moment. Much like CBT, it is short-lived and focused.

Where this therapy differs is that it does not focus as much on changing self-defeating thoughts and behaviors, but more on interpersonal relationships. How does one interact with other important individuals in their life? Are they able to relate to those around them? These are the types of areas that are focused on and explored.

Often used on a one-on-one basis, this therapy focuses on improving communication and the way one relates to others, in order to treat depression. If a specific behavior is causing issues when trying to relate to others, this behavior will be targeted.

FAMILY-FOCUSED THERAPY

First developed to treat bipolar disorder, family-focused therapy (FFT) was designed to help strengthen a patient's relationship with their family. Now used to treat anything from eating disorders to PTSD, families begin to discover how changes in communication can benefit their loved one's recovery.

In order to offer that much-needed support in terms of managing one's illness, family members participate in therapy. This not only offers support but helps to significantly improve and strengthen relationships.

Within therapy, therapists will identify the main issues and conflicts that are occurring within the family. Based on those conflicts, they can better see what may or may not be influencing one's illness. Not only is the patient an area of focus, as therapists sit down with family members to explain what's happening with their loved one's disorder. Education is critical in terms of recovery and support.

This helps family members to understand that hostile reactions towards their loved one's does not help the situation. Although negative emotions may still occur, therapists teach family members how to communicate their emotions in a healthier and more constructive manner.

STRESS INOCULATION TRAINING

This therapy blends behavioral and cognitive aspects with humanistic training techniques. This allows clients to cope more effectively after stressful situations based on the anxiety they feel. This three-phase process encourages clients to use prior coping skills to better adapt.

The first phase is based on personal customization. Clients are interviewed and psychologically tested so that the therapist can create a training process that will benefit that client's needs. This phase is meant to prepare clients to confront their current reactions to stressors.

The second phase focuses on learning new skills and rehearsing these skills. Some of the most common areas of focus are communication skills, problem-solving, self-regulation, and building interpersonal skills. The final phase requires the applications of these skills. Clients have an opportunity to practice their new skills based on a wide range of stressors based on role-playing, modeling, and imagery.

Chapter 6.
Criticisms

Although CBT has been shown to be effective, it does have some weaknesses argued by other professionals in the field. There is no doubt that CBT has been shown to be superior to medication when treating symptoms of anxiety and depression, however, it does suffer from the following weaknesses.

Firstly, CBT focuses on the client and their ability to make changes. Some feel as though this approach is too narrow in that it ignores other external factors such as personal history, family, and wider emotional issues.

It's important to remember that each individual is unique in terms of their mental health and their approach to treatment. CBT is most effective when clients are voluntary and motivated. An individual needs to commit themselves to the process, as their complete co-operation and willingness to change is imperative. Without their effort, the therapist's efforts may be wasted. If a client is unwilling to make changes, CBT can be ineffective. For those who enter treatment thinking that a problem doesn't exist or they're unsure what they want to do about their current issues, it can be tough to make progress. This is when *motivational interviewing* can be helpful, as a stronger relationship is developed between the therapist and client. Once a client is committed, comfortable sharing, and ready to take action, CBT is much more useful.

There's also the possibility that CBT will backfire with certain individuals. Some clients may feel as though they're judged and their distorted thinking is then seen a humanity flaw. For some, this leads to feelings that bad things happen to them because they're bad people, based on their thought patterns. For people like this, symptoms of anxiety can actually worsen and increase anxiety rather than alleviating it.

Another major criticism is that clinical studies for CBT are not double-blind. Since the patient is such an active component of treatment, they are quite aware regarding the group they're in. Although it may be single-blind, in that the rater will not know the type of treatment given, patients nor therapists are blinded to the type of therapy given.

CBT has been criticized for being overly rigid in terms of an educational approach and goal setting. Some are concerned that it does not take into account the big picture, focusing on multiple factors within one's life. Relationships and family issues are not typically addressed. Yes, emotions are taken into account, however, they're not the focal point. For those who are overly emotional, CBT may be less effective regarding change. If they have a strong and immediate emotional reaction, a focus on cognition and behavior may not be the most effective strategy. This is simply because CBT is quite rigid, focusing on thinking more than emotion.

Although CBT can be adapted to a wide range of situations, it's not for everyone. For individuals that suffer from a reoccurring or chronic condition, they may require repeated interventions. For some, they need to address earlier life experiences, as well as issues surrounding their personality or identity. In these cases, they may need to shift their approach to another form of therapy.

ABOUT THE AUTHOR

REBECA FRANKS BEGAN WRITING IN ORDER TO INSPIRE AND CHANGE THE WORLD, ONE READER AT A TIME.

She aims to provide practical tools that anyone can apply into their daily lives. Whether you have hit rock bottom or are simply looking to further enhance your life, she provides informative content to help her readers reach their goals.

She has been studying and applying psychology for over 10 years and met a lot of interesting people along the way. With these writings, Franks wants to keep inspiring others to change for the better.

Printed in Great Britain
by Amazon